WILD ANIMALS

RED PANDAS

BY ABBY DOTY

WWW.APEXEDITIONS.COM

Copyright © 2026 by Apex Editions, Mendota Heights, MN 55120. All rights reserved. No part of this book may be reproduced or utilized in any form or by any means without written permission from the publisher.

Apex is distributed by North Star Editions:
sales@northstareditions.com | 888-417-0195

Produced for Apex by Red Line Editorial.

Photographs ©: Shutterstock Images, cover, 7, 14, 15, 18, 20, 22–23, 24–25, 26–27; Mathias Appel/Flickr, 1, 4–5, 10–11, 16–17, 21; iStockphoto, 6, 8, 29; Dave Pape/Wikimedia Commons, 12–13

Library of Congress Control Number: 2025930924

ISBN
979-8-89250-551-2 (hardcover)
979-8-89250-587-1 (paperback)
979-8-89250-655-7 (ebook pdf)
979-8-89250-623-6 (hosted ebook)

Printed in the United States of America
Mankato, MN
082025

NOTE TO PARENTS AND EDUCATORS

Apex books are designed to build literacy skills in striving readers. Exciting, high-interest content attracts and holds readers' attention. The text is carefully leveled to allow students to achieve success quickly. Additional features, such as bolded glossary words for difficult terms, help build comprehension.

TABLE OF CONTENTS

CHAPTER 1
SMELLY ESCAPE 4

CHAPTER 2
UP IN THE TREES 10

CHAPTER 3
FOOD AND FIGHTING 16

CHAPTER 4
LIFE CYCLE 22

COMPREHENSION QUESTIONS • 28
GLOSSARY • 30
TO LEARN MORE • 31
ABOUT THE AUTHOR • 31
INDEX • 32

CHAPTER 1

SMELLY ESCAPE

A red panda climbs through the trees. She searches for bamboo. Suddenly, a leopard leaps onto a nearby branch.

Red pandas can jump nearly 5 feet (1.5 m) across branches.

Red pandas often stand tall when in danger.

The red panda stands on her back legs. She swipes her claws. But the leopard dodges to the side. Then the leopard jumps toward the red panda.

FAST FACT A red panda uses its tail to help with balance.

Red pandas live near several kinds of leopards, including the snow leopard.

The red panda lets out a stinky smell from below her tail. The leopard backs away. Meanwhile, the red panda races down the tree to safety.

FACE FIRST
Red pandas have **flexible** ankles. That lets the animals climb down trees headfirst. They can move down quickly. And they can look out for **predators** below.

◀ **Only a few animals are able to climb down trees headfirst.**

CHAPTER 2

UP IN THE TREES

Red pandas are small **mammals**. They weigh up to 17 pounds (8 kg). The animals have thick, red fur.

A red panda's tail is about 17 inches (43 cm) long.

Furry paws keep red pandas warm when walking on snow.

Red pandas live in rainy mountain forests. The bottoms of their paws are covered in hair. That helps them grip wet branches and slippery rocks.

FAST FACT

Red pandas have long wrist bones. The bones work like thumbs. So, red pandas can grab things.

Chinese red pandas have striped tails.

There are two kinds of red pandas. They are Himalayan red pandas and Chinese red pandas. Himalayan red pandas are a bit smaller. They also have whiter faces.

Two Types

Both types of red pandas live in the eastern Himalayas. Chinese red pandas mostly live in Myanmar and China. Himalayan red pandas mainly live in Nepal, India, and Bhutan.

The Himalayas are a huge mountain range. The forests there are often cold and windy.

CHAPTER 3

FOOD AND FIGHTING

Red pandas sleep for up to 17 hours a day. The animals are most active during dawn and dusk. They spend much of that time **foraging**.

A red panda may wrap its tail around its body for warmth.

Red pandas are omnivores. They eat mostly bamboo. But they also eat fruit, roots, and insects.

FAST FACT
In one week, a red panda lets out its entire body weight in poop.

Strong jaws and flat teeth help red pandas chew through tough plants.

Red pandas have several predators. They include leopards, jackals, and dholes. Red pandas stay in trees to keep safe.

Dholes are wild dogs that live in central and southeastern Asia.

Fewer than 10,000 red pandas remain in the wild.

HUMAN HARM

Humans cause lots of harm to red pandas. People destroy the animals' forest **habitats**. They build houses and farms there. People also hunt red pandas for their fur.

CHAPTER 4

LIFE CYCLE

Red pandas live alone. But they do come together to **mate**. Females are **pregnant** for about four months.

To find mates, female red pandas follow the smell of males' pee.

A mother has between one and four cubs. At first, the babies are helpless. The mother feeds them milk. After a few months, the cubs begin to **explore**.

COZY NESTS
Female red pandas create nests for their cubs. They use holes in trees or stumps. They line their nests with plants. The cubs stay inside for months.

Red pandas open their eyes two to three weeks after birth.

The cubs start eating bamboo after about five months. They leave their mother when they are about one year old. Six months later, they begin having their own babies.

FAST FACT

Red pandas live for about 10 years in the wild.

Female red pandas care for their cubs without help from males.

COMPREHENSION QUESTIONS

Write your answers on a separate piece of paper.

1. Write a few sentences explaining the main ideas of Chapter 4.

2. What feature of red pandas do you find most interesting? Why?

3. What is one country where Chinese red pandas live?
    - **A.** India
    - **B.** Nepal
    - **C.** Myanmar

4. At what age can a red panda begin having its own babies?
    - **A.** 12 months
    - **B.** 18 months
    - **C.** 10 years

5. What does **dodges** mean in this book?

*She swipes her claws. But the leopard **dodges** to the side.*

    A. avoids
    B. fights
    C. freezes

6. What does **omnivores** mean in this book?

*Red pandas are **omnivores**. They eat mostly bamboo. But they also eat fruit, roots, and insects.*

    A. animals that eat only plants
    B. animals that eat only animals
    C. animals that eat both plants and animals

Answer key on page 32.

GLOSSARY

explore
To search or move through an area.

flexible
Easy to bend or move.

foraging
Searching for food.

habitats
The places where animals normally live.

mammals
Animals that have hair and produce milk for their young.

mate
To form a pair and come together to have babies.

predators
Animals that hunt and eat other animals.

pregnant
When one or more babies are growing in an animal's body.

BOOKS

Gish, Melissa. *Red Pandas.* Creative Education, 2024.

Grack, Rachel. *Red Pandas.* Bellwether Media, 2024.

O'Brien, Cynthia. *Giant Panda vs. Red Panda.* Kaleidoscope Publishing, 2025.

ONLINE RESOURCES

Visit **www.apexeditions.com** to find links and resources related to this title.

ABOUT THE AUTHOR

Abby Doty is a writer, editor, and booklover from Minnesota.

INDEX

B
bamboo, 4, 19, 26
Bhutan, 15

C
China, 15
claws, 6
climbing, 4, 9
cubs, 24, 26

F
foraging, 16
fur, 10, 21

H
habitats, 21
Himalayas, 15

I
India, 15

L
leopards, 4, 6, 9, 20

M
mammals, 10
Myanmar, 15

N
Nepal, 15
nests, 24

P
paws, 13
predators, 9, 20

T
tail, 7, 9
trees, 4, 9, 20, 24

ANSWER KEY:
1. Answers will vary; 2. Answers will vary; 3. C; 4. B; 5. A; 6. C

32